FUN FACTS

D0128182

Ripley's
Believe It or Not!®
Kids

& SILLY STORIES

Editor Jessica Firpi
Designers Michelle Foster, Josh Surprenant, Jessica Firpi
Reprographics Juice Creative

ISBN 978-1-60991-142-3 (US)

Library of Congress Control Number: 2015942040

For information regarding permission, write to
VP Intellectual Property
Ripley Entertainment Inc.
7576 Kingspointe Parkway, Suite 188
Orlando, Florida, 32819
Email: publishing@ripleys.com
www.ripleys.com/books

Manufactured in China
in June/2015
1st printing

PUBLISHER'S NOTE
While every effort has been made to verify the accuracy
of the entries in this book, the Publishers cannot be held
responsible for any errors contained in the work. They
would be glad to receive any information from readers.

WARNING
Some of the stunts and activities in this book are
undertaken by experts and should not be attempted by
anyone without adequate training and supervision.

FUN FACTS & SILLY STORIES

Ripley's
Believe It or Not!®
Kids

4

What do you do when you run out of art canvas?

Use bananas, of course!

4

Former chef Elisa Roche is a banana artist and shares her creations on her Instagram, @funwithfruit!

5

Babies have taste buds

I know they are in here!

in their cheeks.

Dogs don't feel guilt—they just feel sad that their owner is yelling at them.

Igloos can be more than 100 degrees warmer inside than outside.

In China, giant panda mom Juxiao could only take care of two of her triplets at a time.

When they were finally reunited, Juxiao hugged all her babies tightly.

On a casual stroll, a California couple discovered a pot of buried gold coins worth more than

10 Million Dollars

I'm purrrfect for politics!

A cat named Stubbs has been the mayor of an Alaskan town for **16 years!**

The largest T. rex tooth discovered was **12 inches (30.5 cm) long!**

A beaver's teeth **NEVER** stop growing.

Ten-year-old Noah Cordle thought he had stepped on a crab, but when he looked down, he discovered a rare

14,000-year-old Clovis point arrowhead!

DO I LOOK LIKE A CRAB?!!

Norway knighted a penguin named Nils Olav!

In the Austrian Alps, Matteo Walch became best friends with a colony of MARMOTS!

Rock candy was once used as medicine.

Alligator teeth are hollow.

There's a black hole that eats gas in an amount equivalent to

100 billion hot dogs per minute!

In 1904, snack sellers serving ice cream ran out of dishes, so they rolled up a waffle—and the cone was born!

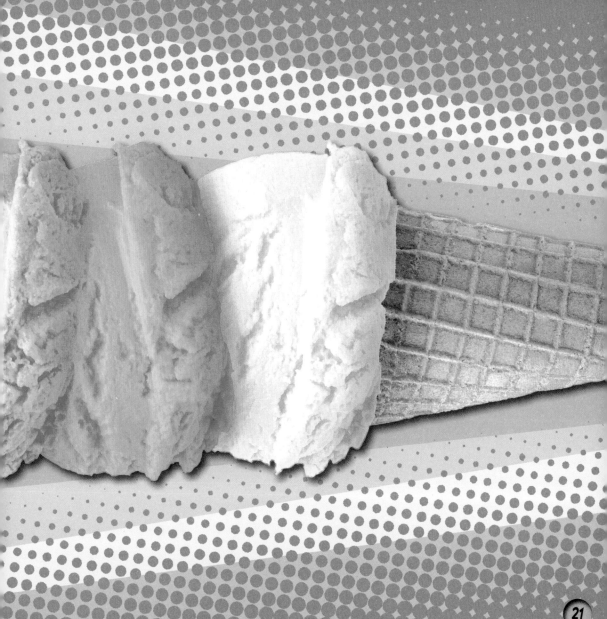

Believe it or not, pinball was banned in New York City from 1942 to 1976!

Hippopotomonstrosesquippedaliophobia is the fear of long words.

The bill of a platypus feels like suede!

$$123 - 45 - 67 + 89 = 100.$$

$$123 + 4 - 5 + 67 - 89 = 100.$$

$$123 - 4 - 5 - 6 - 7 + 8 - 9 = 100.$$

$$1 + 23 - 4 + 5 + 6 + 78 - 9 = 100.$$

When playing, male puppies will often let female puppies win.

A grandfather in Japan used an old oil barrel to make his grandson sidecars shaped like a panda and Thomas the Tank Engine!

In California, Zeus the blind screech owl fascinates everyone with his amazing eyes that look like the universe!

JUST KEEP SWIMMING!

Some shark species must keep swimming or else they'll DROWN.

Biology teacher Ana Retamero captured these ordinary orchids appearing otherworldly!

In China, a posh dog walked in the snow wearing a warm mink coat and boots.

Raven George, a captive raven at the Tower of London, was fired for munching on TV antennas.

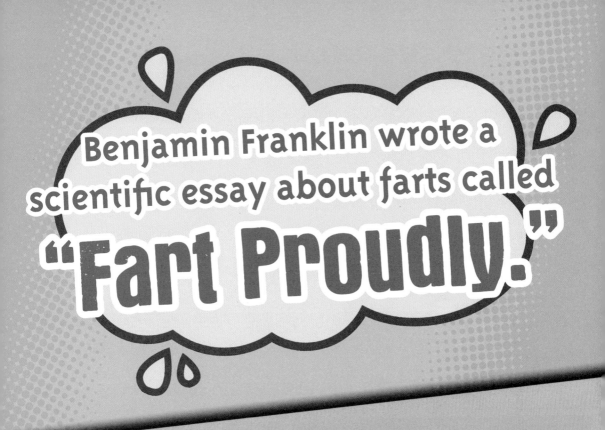

Benjamin Franklin wrote a scientific essay about farts called "Fart Proudly."

Chimpanzees have a better short-term memory than humans!

Earthquakes can turn water into gold.

Cheetahs can't roar!

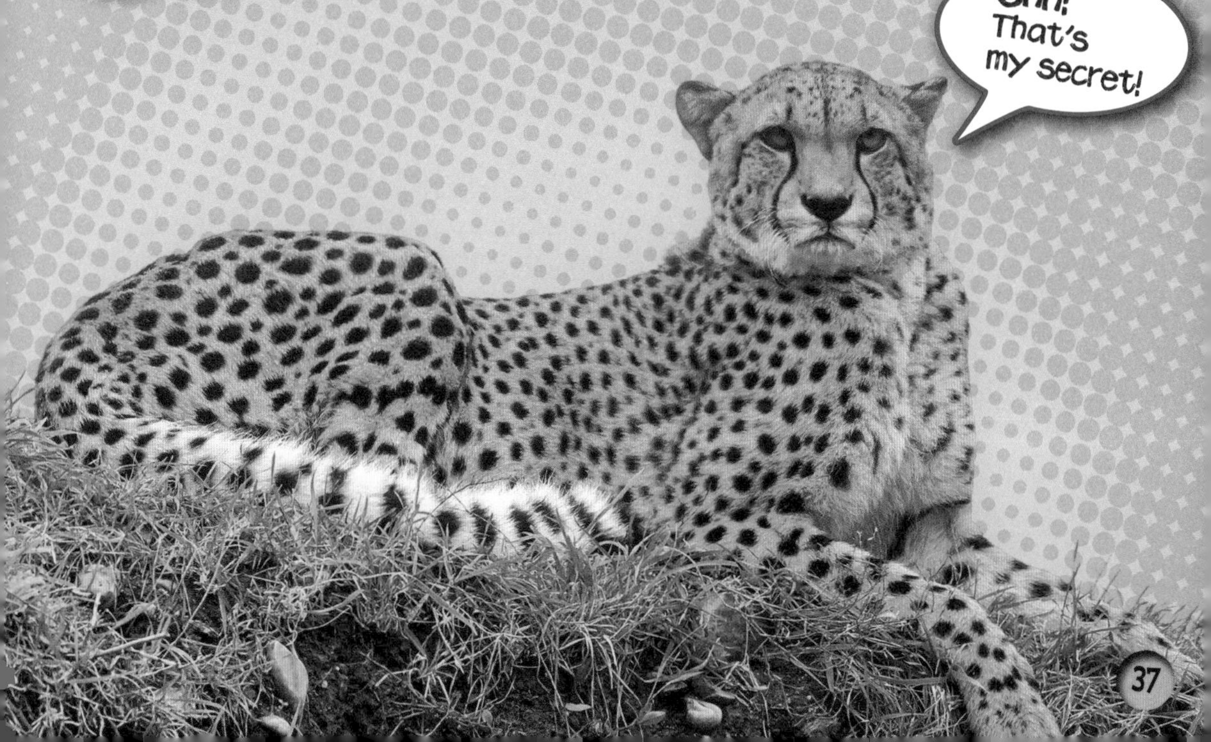

A pizzeria in Vienna, Austria, is home to a **giant disco ball** pizza oven!

It even rotates!

A family in Derbyshire, England, often shares breakfast with Joe the camel, seen here eating a bowl of cereal and munching on fruit.

Japanese macaques have learned to steal coins to buy tasty snacks from vending machines!

It can snow without any clouds in the sky!

A group of hummingbirds is called a "glittering."

The violet snail travels the ocean on a homemade raft of bubbles.

ROAR
into
Hanukkah
with a
dinosaur
MENORAH!

Frank Epperson invented the Popsicle when he was just 11 years old.

Viruses can get viruses.

cough!

Ancient people created the first ice skates out of

BONE!

Some people snore louder than a

VACUUM CLEANER.

BABY-RITO!

Who needs an ordinary baby blanket when you could have a burrito blanket! Designer Corinne Leroux creates these unique baby blankets.

WEIRD, THIS IS

Strangely, the folds in this pig's head resemble iconic *Star Wars* character Yoda.

FRIENDS ARE FURR-EVER!

Newborn Alia cuddles, sleeps, and plays with her best friend Daisy —a sloth! Alia's parents also keep a kangaroo, an anteater, a sugar glider, and a cat.

In Mexico, artists can pay their taxes with **ARTWORK!**

Mars is populated entirely by robots— **7** to be exact.

A sneakerhead is someone who collects sneakers.

The national anthem of Spain has no words.

AÑA

SECOND HELPINGS

Anteaters never destroy an anthill so they can eat there again.

You cannot work in Antarctica unless you have your wisdom teeth and appendix removed first.

Antarctic weather is so hostile that a medical evacuation is **impossible.**

UPSIDE-DOWN!

Tourists in Shanghai
can check out a
house built

Dancing on
the ceiling

62

63

Sarimin the long-tailed macaque entertains tourists in Indonesia, who flock to watch him perform stunts on his miniature motor bike.

PARIS PROTESTERS

Protesting farmers* showed up at the Eiffel Tower — with their flocks of sheep!

*The farmers were opposing the government's protection of wolves, which kill too many animals.

The average fashion show is only 10 minutes long!

The word gypsy is short for "Egyptian," but gypsies originally came from India!

Police officers in India receive an allowance for growing mustaches.

They just have to be inspected by the chief of police first!

CYBER-SQUIRREL!

A mom in England created a fun backyard feeder inspired by *Doctor Who's* Cybermen.

Believe it or not, only licensed electricians may change a light bulb in Victoria, Australia.

Victoria

There is a flower in Japan and China

whose petals become translucent when it rains.

Andean bear twins Tupa and Sonco were born Christmas Day, 2013, so they happily opened their Christmas and birthday gift at the zoo in Frankfurt, Germany.

YOU'RE SO NOSY!

Bob Carter snapped this photo of a weeping willow tree that looks just like a nose!

Sniff sniff

A designer created a SELFIE HAT for London Fashion Week!

In Australia, there are more kangaroos than people.

Montreal is home to Canada's first mermaid school!

Both species of water deer are native to Asia, and their amazingly long canine teeth have given them a quirky nickname:

Vampire Deer!

Best friends come in all shapes and sizes—just look at Gerald the giraffe and Zeberdee the zebra!

To create the "Street View" of the Liwa Oasis desert, Google hired a camel named Raffia!

You can only see a rainbow if your back is to the sun.

Canadians buy and eat macaroni and cheese more than any other country!

ANATIDAEPHOBIA

is the fear that somewhere, somehow, a duck is watching you.

CHEEKY FISHY

Underwater photographer Regan Mizuguchi was all set to take a selfie off Hawaii's Kohala coast when a pufferfish photo-bombed him!

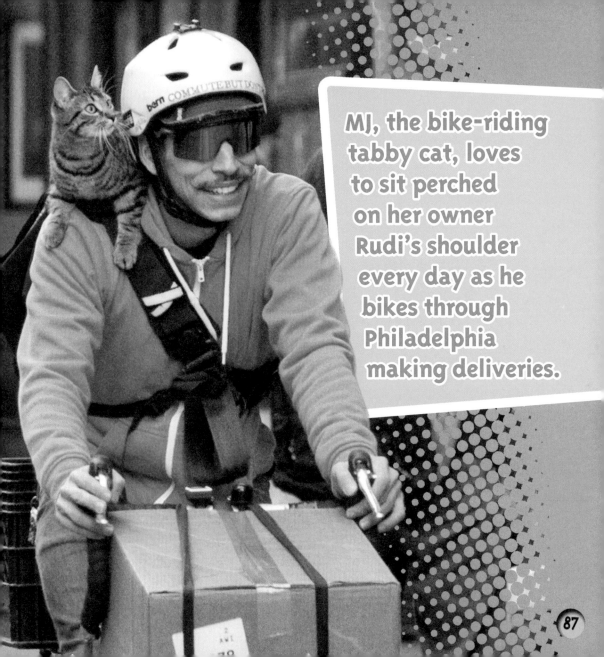

MJ, the bike-riding tabby cat, loves to sit perched on her owner Rudi's shoulder every day as he bikes through Philadelphia making deliveries.

Nagasaki Bio Park in Japan has a road built for guinea pigs!

Beep Beep!

The guinea pigs commute from one play area to another using this cute highway!

Jackie Dye from Springfield, Michigan, sells crochet mermaid tail blankets!

Send waterproof postcards home from the world's first underwater post office!

VANUATU & OVERSEAS
CLEARED DAILY

92

A small town in Spain installed the world's first **public dog toilet!**

Camels once roamed the Canadian Arctic!

ROBO-CROC!

"Longlong," the 21-foot (6.4-m) crocodile robot, surprised people on his way to Crocodile Park in Manila, Phillipines.

In Botswana, a few curious meerkats perched on and around photographer Will Burrard-Lucas and his cameras.

There is an island in Japan
populated entirely by RABBITS.
It is called Usaga Jima,
or Rabbit Island.

PEDALING MANTIS!

This unassuming praying mantis jumped onto a curled plant and looked just like he was riding a bicycle.

The Amazon rain forest supplies one-fifth of the world's oxygen!

Babies don't shed tears until they are at least one month old.

GO BANANAS!

The International Banana Museum in California is the world's largest collection devoted to any one fruit.

Hamburgers got their name from the German city of Hamburg.

The chemical compound used in vanilla flavoring and "new car smell" comes from

BEAVERS!

FINISH

Bob the burrowing owl dominated at London Zoo's Animal Athletes in Action demonstration, running his signature 100-cm sprint.

In South Africa, five-year-old Finn Johnson brought his A-game to a soccer match he had with **two ELEPHANTS each weighing 3 tons!**

Stacey Wallace took a **SELFIE** with a GROUND SQUIRREL in Canada! She coaxed it out of its hole with nuts.

GRITS FESTIVAL

Roll around in traditional Southern goodness during the Rolling in the Grits contest at the World Grits Festival in South Carolina.

A baby guinea pig can run after being alive just

Go speed Racer, Go!

3 hours!

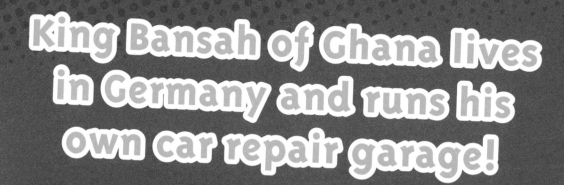

King Bansah of Ghana lives in Germany and runs his own car repair garage!

110

Scientists discovered a new frog species that does not croak! Instead it groans and makes coughing noises.

A giant dog named Joker and a small pony named Tigger are best friends.

Using paint and scrap materials, staff at the Margam Country Park in Wales spruced up a few boring hay bales to look like farm animals.

By practicing the right techniques, you can control your dreams!

Despite being slow on land, sloths are actually great swimmers!

More than 30 million people in China live in caves!

In the Middle East, camels wear funky

LYCRA SUITS

to help them run faster in races.

117

Creator Jim Rodda outfitted a warrior Barbie with a 3D-printed cat chariot!

A leopon is a cross between a leopard and a lioness.

+ = A leopon

There are 169,518,829,100,544,000,000,000,000 ways to play the first ten moves of any chess game.

The entire country of Liechtenstein can be rented for

$70,000

a day.

THE TIME TRAVEL MART

There is a time travel store in Los Angeles, California, that sells things you might need for a trip through time.

Mammoth Chunks

Robot Milk

Leeches

Time Travel Sickness Pills

FOXY FEAST

A famished fox plunged headfirst into hard snow while trying to catch a meal!

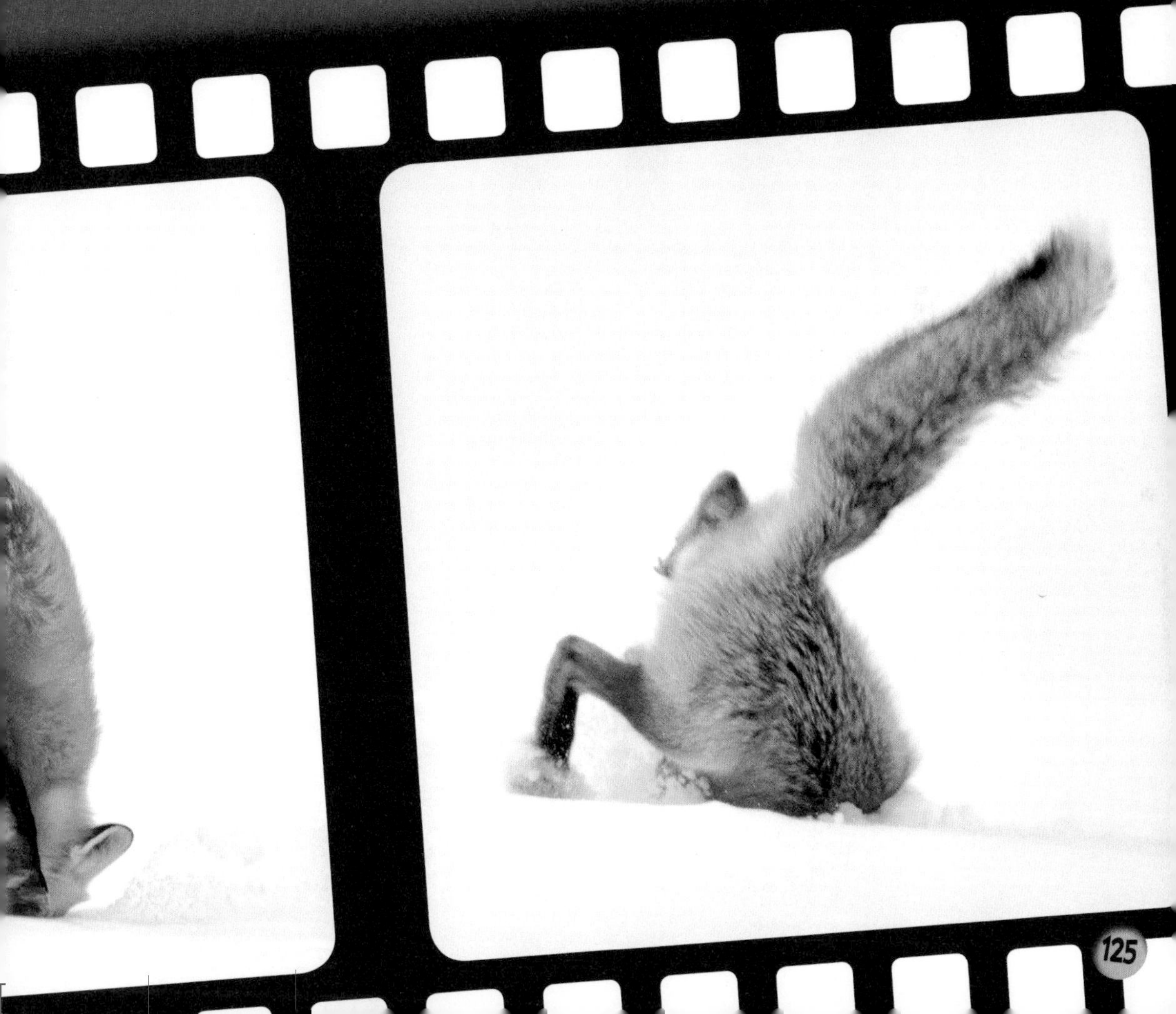

SKY-NOCEROS

Endangered rhinos sometimes need help being moved to safer habitats. Comfortable upside-down helicopter rides help them reach their new homes.

Only male turkeys gobble! Female turkeys click.

Chinese checkers was invented in GERMANY and has nothing to do with the game of checkers.

Some giant tarantulas keep tiny frogs as pets!

The frogs eat any insects that might harm the spider's eggs, and the spider keeps the frog safe in return.

129

MEET PRINGLE!

This charming 4-year-old bearded dragon isn't afraid to let loose.

Artistic alpacas at Toft Farm in England were **DYED DIFFERENT COLORS** after a close shearing.

Parrot fish sleep in cocoons made of their own mucus!

In 2012, a 10-year-old student in Missouri accidentally discovered a new molecule —

TETRANITRATOXYCARBON!

HONEY WILL NEVER SPOIL.

Americans consume **10 BILLION** donuts a year.

Sweet potatoes and YAMS
are not the same thing!

There are no wild tigers in Africa!

These adorable dormice from Russia climbed a dried reed to cuddle and laugh even after their home was destroyed by loggers.

LIP SERVICE

Makeup artist Laura Jenkinson delights her Instagram followers with more than 50 cartoon masterpieces she's painted on her mouth and chin!

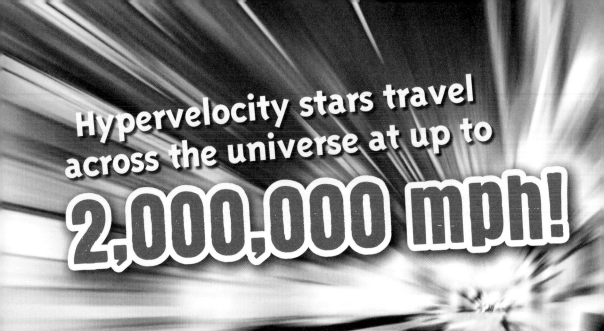

Hypervelocity stars travel across the universe at up to

2,000,000 mph!

Dogs are banned from Antarctica!

THE WORLD'S QUIETEST PLACE IS -9 DECIBELS

It's a chamber so quiet you can hear your own blood flow!

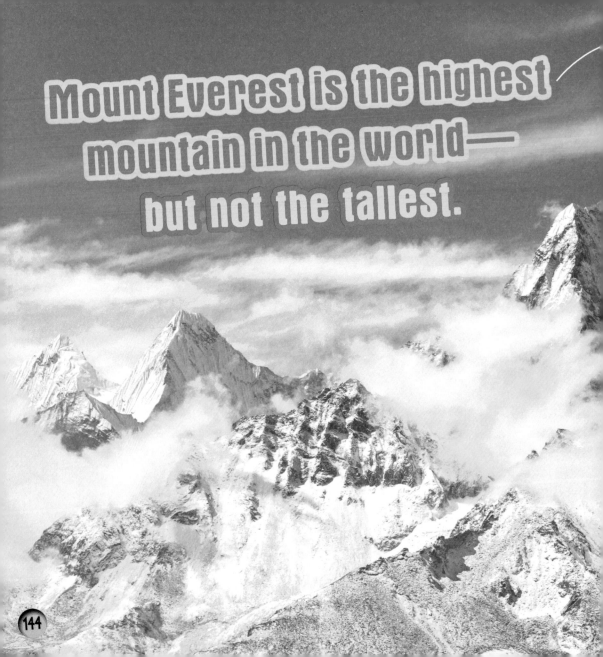

Mount Everest is the highest mountain in the world—
but not the tallest.

If you were able to place the planet Saturn

In a big bowl of water, it would float!

SCIENTISTS DISCOVERED A TINY SPECIES OF FROG THAT IS SMALLER THAN A DIME!

ACTUAL SIZE

Human teeth are just as strong as shark teeth.

CAT-ERPILLAR

Caterpillars come in all shapes and sizes, but a few look super silly. The Chinese bush brown caterpillar looks like Hello Kitty!

Hey, you want to play?

Penny the silkie chicken and Roo the two-legged chihuahua love to meet and play with anyone who stops by the Duluth Animal Hospital in Georgia.

At a zoo in Holland, Snor the walrus squirted a jet of water at a girl who got too close.

151

CUDDLY
CUBS

Little lion cubs in Kenya convinced their mother to tickle and play with them instead of leaving them to find food.

In Indonesia, Krisdian Wardana managed to take a quick snap of a cheeky snail crawling over a lizard's head!

Oh, that feels nice!

Yakutian cattle can tolerate freezing temperatures in part thanks to their thick winter coats.

It's hot in here!

Roller Coasters

can make your organs move around in your body!

156

Fingernails grow about three to four times faster than toenails.

Believe it or not, there are over 65 kinds of bacteria... in your BELLY BUTTON!

Ahmad El Abi has stuffed his curly locks with everything

from Legos and spaghetti noodles, to bubbles and lollipops.

There's a wild animal in east Asia called the raccoon dog—it looks like a raccoon but is really **a dog!**

Hummingbird moths

move just like hummingbirds and use their long tongues to snack on flower nectar!

Canada has more lakes than the rest of the world!

Looking to build sand castles on the beach this summer?

The competition
is fierce!

You can tell the temperature by counting a cricket's chirps.

1... 2... 3... 4...

chirp... chirp... chirp... chirp...

RIBBIT! RIBBIT! RIBBIT!

Some frogs get noisier just before it rains.

Extreme heat can make train tracks **BEND.**

These clever winter squirrels posed for the camera while looking for the nuts photographer Vadim Trunov hid inside a few snowballs!

Osage orange fruits can be used to repel Cockroaches!

RUN!

SCURRY!

Follow my lead.

Seahorse couples start each day by dancing together!

Soccer-playing **ROBOTS** compete at the annual Robocup!

Wildfires can sometimes create tornadoes made of fire called

FIRE WHIRLS.

When listening to music, your heart beat speeds up or slows down depending on the song's tempo.

You could grow asparagus on Mars!

These fascinating sea slugs resemble little sheep!

PATTY THE PAINTING DONKEY

dons her signature red beret and wields a paintbrush in her mouth to create unique masterpieces!

Early explorers used watermelons as canteens.

New Yorkers bite people 10 times more often than sharks do.

178

BLEAK BLUFFS

Australia has a mountain called **Mt. Disappointment** and another mountain called **Mt. Terrible.**

A group of ferrets is called a business.

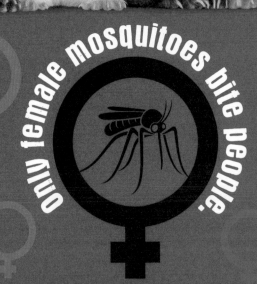

Only female mosquitoes bite people.

A jeweller engraved a secret message on Abraham Lincoln's pocket watch that was not discovered until 2009— 140 years later!

Male elephants are called bulls, females are called cows, and baby elephants are called calves.

SNOWY OWL FACTS

This happy owl was actually caught having a hearty yawn!

Snowy owl parents are highly territorial and will even defend their nests against wolves!

There's a golf club on the border of Sweden and Finland

where half the holes are in one country...

...and half in the other.

Multiplying 21,978 by 4 reverses the order of the numbers: 87,912.

Penguins can't taste fish!

There is no such thing as a panther! Panthers are just black cougars, jaguars, and leopards.

Artist Prudence Staite fashioned some of the United Kingdom's most famous landmarks...

Cheddar cheese Stonehenge chunks!

out of FOOD!

Check out this Big Ben made from peanut butter and jelly sandwiches!

SUGAR RUSH

This public art fir tree decorated like an upside-down ice cream cone charmed everyone at the Gorky Park in Moscow, Russia.

CATWALKS

In Bedfordshire, England, Milly Moo the cat walks William Dutton to preschool every day.

The rafflesia flower smells like ROTTEN MEAT!

The builders of Japan's Nijo Castle created floors that chirp when you step on them to prevent sneaky intruders.

Monkeys, miniature horses, and even potbellied pigs can qualify as "emotional support animals" for US airline passengers.

CHINA FACTS!

The mortar used to bind the Great Wall's stones was made with sticky rice.

In China, you can eat green-bean-flavored ice pops!

In ancient China, soldiers sometimes wore armor made from paper!

There is a wild cat in southern China that sometimes communicates by spitting.

197

M&M's were created so soldiers could enjoy chocolate without it melting.

Leonardo Da Vinci used to buy caged animals at the market just to set them FREE.

When threatened, wild ferrets will

DANCE.

Umbrellas
were originally created
to provide shade
from the sun —

not to protect us from rain!

VEGE-LIFE

Fruits and vegetables don't die the minute they are harvested but continue to react to their environment for days.

Oysters can change their gender!

Humans spend **25 years** of their lives sleeping!

CRITTERS WITH ATTITUDE

A wet koala and a sassy hare stick out their tongues in one kooky display. What are they really trying to say?

White chocolate isn't

technically chocolate.

HAKUNA MATATA

Named after the famous cartoon characters in Disney's *The Lion King*, Timon the meerkat and Pumbaa the micro pig are close pals!

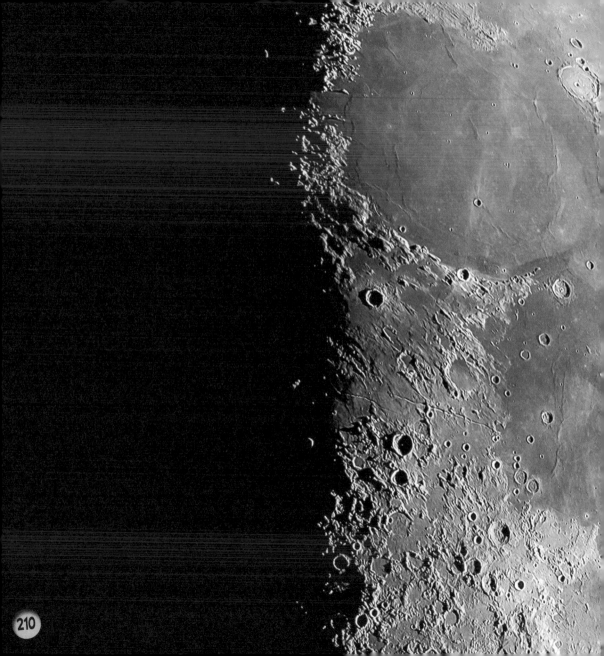

There is high-speed Internet on the Moon!

Mexico's 34th president served for less than an hour before he QUIT!

There is a bat in New Zealand that spends the majority of its life walking on the ground!

Believe it or not, the "S" in former US president Harry S. Truman's name does not stand for a middle name — just "S"!

Sam Stefani spent about £10,000 ($14,800) building up his epic Spice Girls collection.

"Big Ben" is not the name of the London clock tower — but the massive bell inside it!

TIMM SCHNEIDER'S LIVELY STREET ART WATCHES PASSERSBY WITH THEIR BEADY EYES.

TRASH-MAN!

Meet superhero Mangetsu-man (Mr. Full Moon) who cleans up the streets of Tokyo, Japan, using nothing but a broom and dustpan!

INDEX

PHOTO CREDITS

138-139 MIROSLAV HLAVKO / CATERS NEWS; 140-141 Laura Jenkinson; 142 (t) © csl945 - Shutterstock.com, (b) © MilsiArt - Shutterstock.com; 144-145 © saiko3p - Shutterstock.com; 146 (c) © Coprid - Shutterstock .com, © alexokokok - Shutterstock.com; 147 (t) © Pete Spiro - Shutterstock.com; 148 Melvyn Yeo; 149 © dean bertoncelj - Shutterstock.com; 150 Alicia Williams; 151 NATALIA PAKLINA / CATERS NEWS; 152-153 Jagdeep Rajput/ Solent News/Rex/REX USA; 154 Krisdian Wardana/Rex/REX USA; 155 BOLOT BOCHKAREV / CATERS NEWS; 156 © SIHASAKPRACHUM - Shutterstock.com; 158 (l) AHMAD EL ABI / CATERS NEWS, (r) AHMAD EL ABI / CATERS NEWS; 159 AHMAD EL ABI / CATERS NEWS; 160 © Stanislav Duben - Shutterstock.com; 161 © Bildagentur Zoonar GmbH - Shutterstock.com; 162-163 © karamysh - Shutterstock.com; 164 REPORTERS / CATERS NEWS; 165 JOO HENG TAN / CATERS NEWS; 166 (t) © Panachai Cherdchucheep - Shutterstock.com, (b) © Chros - Shutterstock.com; 167 © PanicAttack - Shutterstock.com; 168-169 Vadim Trunov/Solent News; 170 (c) © Alex Zabusik - Shutterstock.com, (b) © sumroeng chinnapan - Shutterstock.com; 171 © slalomgigante - Shutterstock.com; 172-173 TU/e, Bart van Overbeeke; 174 © MichaelWarrenPix - iStock.com; 175 (l) © Vectomart - Shutterstock.com, (r) © Kuttelvaserova Stuchelova - Shutterstock.com; 176 RANDI ANG / CATERS NEWS; 177 ADAM HARNETT / CATERS NEWS; 178 (t) © indigolotos - Shutterstock.com, (c) © Nattika - Shutterstock.com; 180 (t) © Eric Isselee - Shutterstock.com, (b) © VKA - Shutterstock.com; 181 © Ferenc Cegledi - Shutterstock.com; 182-183 © Anup Shah/naturepl.com; 184-185 © James.Pintar - Shutterstock.com; 186-187 © Italianvideophotoagency - Shutterstock.com; 188 (r) © yyang - Shutterstock.com; 189 © Volodymyr Burdiak - Shutterstock.com; 190 Caters News Agency; 191 Caters News Agency; 192 © ITAR-TASS Photo Agency / Alamy; 193 HARRY WHITEHEAD / CATERS NEWS; 194 © Nokuro - Shutterstock.com; 196-197 © Songquan Deng - Shutterstock.com; 198 (t) © Cyrick - Shutterstock.com; 199 (r) © VitCOM Photo - Shutterstock.com, (bgd) © eyedear - Shutterstock.com; 200-201 © Alfonso de Tomas - Shutterstock.com; 202 © sunabesyou - Shutterstock.com; 203 © Picsfive - Shutterstock.com; 204-205 SIMON LITTEN / CATERS NEWS; 205 MATTHEW GRAHAM WILKINSON / CATERS NEWS; 206-207 © MaraZe - Shutterstock.com; 208-209 ADAM HARNETT / CATERS; 210-211 © Matipon - Shutterstock.com; 212 © Filipe Frazao - Shutterstock.com; 213 © nemlaza - Shutterstock.com; 214-215 LIZ GREGG / CATERS NEWS; 216-217 © NAN728 - Shutterstock.com; 218 (b/l) TIMM SCHNEIDER / CATERS NEWS, (bgd) TIMM SCHNEIDER / CATERS NEWS; 219 REUTERS/Issei Kato

Key: t = top, b = bottom, c = center, l = left, r = right, bgd = background

All other photos are from Ripley Entertainment Inc. and Shutterstock.com. Every attempt has been made to acknowledge correctly and contact copyright holders and we apologize in advance for any unintentional errors or omissions, which will be corrected in future editions.

We hope you enjoyed the book!

FUN FACTS
Ripley's
Believe It or Not!
Kids
3 SILLY STORIES

Have you seen books one, two, and three? They're packed with even more fun facts and silly stories!